BRAIN SURFING
& 31
OTHER AWESOME QUALITIES OF ADHD

REAL LIFE STORIES AND EXAMPLES
ABOUT THE POSITIVE ATTRIBUTES OF
LIVING WITH ADHD

BY

LAURIE DUPAR, PMHNP, RN, PCC

Brain Surfing & 31 Other Awesome Qualities of ADHD

© 2011 Laurie Dupar, Coaching for ADHD

ISBN: 978-0-615-52213-5

All rights reserved. No portion of this book may be reproduced mechanically, electronically, or by any other means, including photocopying, without written permission of the publisher. It is illegal to copy this book, post it to a website, or distribute it by any other means without permission from the publisher.

The purpose of this book is to educate and entertain. The author and/or publisher do not guarantee that anyone following these techniques, suggestions, tips, ideas, or strategies will become successful. The author and/or publisher shall have neither liability nor responsibility to anyone with respect to any loss or damage caused, or alleged to be caused, directly or indirectly by the information contained in this book.

Publisher: Laurie Dupar, Granite Bay, CA

Cover Design by LivingYourMessage.com
Copywriting by www.writeassociate.com

Here is what people are saying about

Brain Surfing & 31 Other Awesome Qualities of ADHD

Dear Laurie

I just read your book *"Brain Surfing and 31 Awesome Qualities of ADHD"*, and I just wanted to say "thank you."

I am discovering more and more the strengths and positive qualities that come along with ADHD. I have been getting bogged down and depressed by focusing on all the annoying struggles of having ADHD. Your book articulates those strengths in a way that's inspired me as much as, if not more than, anything else I've read or heard.

~David Sloan, Columbia, SC

Laurie,

Okay, I just read this book and it is amazing! I had tears in my eyes through much of the book. It's hard to describe how wonderful it is to see all the positive aspects of ADD, especially after years of beating myself up over many of these same things. You are an incredibly gifted person and it was a thrill to read this Laurie. Thank you so much for everything!

~Regina Hertel, San Diego, California

Is This Book For You?

If you are someone who has been diagnosed with ADHD or who cares about someone diagnosed with ADHD, you know how challenging life can be. Life with ADHD is a 24-hour, seven-day–a-week adventure. This book is for you!

Unfortunately, the majority of focus on ADHD is on the "negative" aspects, or the challenges, struggles and problems that people with ADHD experience. Rarely are the positive attributes of ADHD highlighted, appreciated or celebrated.

This book is a dedication to all people living with ADHD and touches on some of those amazing qualities they possess. Having worked for nearly nine years exclusively with people with ADHD, I am convinced that these amazing attributes are the other side of the coin, so to speak; they are the assets and personal talents that enrich our world. I have chosen to highlight 32 of those qualities, although many more exist. The examples in this book are from my real-life experience of living with, loving and working with persons with ADHD. I know there are many more amazing qualities; in fact, I would love to hear about your amazing ADHD qualities!

Go to my Coaching for ADHD Facebook fan page at: http://www.facebook.com/CoachingforADHD, click "Like" and tell me about your positive ADHD qualities!

Brain Surfing & 31 Other Awesome Qualities

Contents

Who is Laurie Dupar? ix
Acknowledgements & Dedication xi

Awesome Qualities of ADHD

Brain Surfing 1
Out of the Box Thinker 5
Creative 9
Fun to be With & Life of the Party 13
Sees Details Others Miss 17
Innovative 21
Humorous 25
Inspiring 29
Resourceful 33
Highly Sensitive 37
Able to Hyper-focus 41
Musically Intuitive 45
Single-Minded Pursuit of a Goal 49
Adventurous 53
Intelligent 57
Can Talk…A LOT 61
Multi-tasker & Productive 65

Contents - Continued

Problem Solver 69
Able to Live in the Moment 73
Willing to Take Risks 77
High Energy 81
Curious 85
Imaginative 89
Tenacious & Resilient 93
Unique 97
Good Negotiator 101
Charming 105
Never Bored & Never Boring 109
Parting Thoughts 113

Contact Laurie Dupar 115

Who is Laurie Dupar?

Laurie Dupar grew up in the Pacific Northwest and now lives in Northern California where she specializes in coaching persons with ADHD.

Her education and background as a trained Psychiatric Mental Health Nurse Practitioner (PMHNP) and Senior Certified ADHD Coach (SCAC) make her uniquely suited to guide persons struggling with attentional challenges through the maze of understanding and appreciating their ADHD/ADD brains. Working with Laurie, clients are finally able to utilize specific strategies that work with their brain style in order to stop the chaos, get things done and accomplish their goals.

Laurie's unique approach includes acknowledging the very real challenges of ADHD, along with her personal appreciation for the uniqueness that persons with ADHD have. In fact, several of her family members have either been diagnosed with ADHD or have "ADD characteristics".

Laurie is also a co-author and editor of the #1 Amazon bestseller and resource book for people with ADHD entitled, *365 ways to succeed with ADHD*. You can purchase it yourself on Amazon.com.

To find out more about how to finally understand and minimize your ADHD challenges by focusing more on your ADHD positive qualities, visit Laurie's website at www.CoachingforADHD.com

Acknowledgements
&
Dedication

My heartfelt appreciation to the following people for being big believers in my dreams:

- To my husband, Dana, for never saying "no".

- To my children, Graham, Joanna, Blake and Michelle, who inspire me every day to be a better person.

And, *especially* to all of my amazing clients who have taught me more about ADHD/ADD than any book I could ever read! I continue to be honored and privileged to be part of your life.

■ ■ ■

This book is dedicated to all my past, present and future clients. Thank you!

"Everybody is a genius. But if you judge a fish by its ability to climb a tree, it will live its whole life believing that it is stupid."

~Albert Einstein

Awesome ADHD Quality #1
Brain Surfing

"These thoughts did not come in any verbal formulation. I rarely think in words at all. A thought comes, and I may try to express it in words afterward."

~Albert Einstein

Brain Surfing

"Brain surfing" is a term I first heard used by one of my clients. She was describing the way it feels when her brain jumps from topic to topic or thought to thought.

This ability to brain surf is frequently experienced by persons with ADHD, especially when they find themselves bored or doing something not very interesting. Although the thoughts that come up when brain surfing can sometimes distract people with ADHD from the current subject at hand, it strikes me as their brain's amazing ability to keep itself occupied in the midst of a more boring situation.

Just think…people with ADHD can take advantage of their natural brain surfing qualities, and NEVER BE BORED AGAIN!

Awesome ADHD Quality #2
Out of the Box Thinker

"Always think outside the box and embrace opportunities that appear, wherever they might be."

~Lakshmi Mittal

Out of the Box Thinker

It seems that in this day and age, everyone is spouting the benefits of being an "out of the box thinker", including the advances possible in academics, business and science when people allow their minds to imagine unconventional and never-before-considered thoughts or ideas. Actually, people with ADHD have had this amazing, sought-after unconventional thought quality nailed for some time!

As an ADHD Coach and specialist who works with clients of all ages, some of my most amazing clients are students. The following story is about one student who is definitely an "out of the box thinker"!

Across the board, remembering to take their medications is a struggle people with ADHD share. Many will try setting an alarm or putting the medication where they can see it as a way to remind themselves to take it. One of my students, a young man just finishing up grade school, came up with a completely "out of the box" way of reminding himself to take his medication each morning.

Each night, lying in his bed, this "out of the box thinker" would first try and remind himself to take his medication in the morning by saying it over and over in his head before he fell asleep. However, no matter his determination the night before, he knew that in the morning he might forget or get distracted. So, each night, this clever young man, while lying in bed, would take one of his bed pillows and throw it across the room so it would block his door.

In the morning when he woke up and went to leave his room, the presence of the pillow, along with the maneuvering needed to move it out of his way, would remind him why it was there. He would pick up the pillow on his way out of his room, toss it back on his bed and go downstairs to take his medication. Definitely, "out of the box thinking", at its finest!

Awesome ADHD Quality #3
Creative

"I like nonsense; it wakes up the brain cells. Fantasy is a necessary ingredient in living; it's a way of looking at life through the wrong end of a telescope. Which is what I do, and that enables you to laugh at life's realities.

~Theodore Geisel

Creative

Creativity reigns supreme for people with ADHD! If there is a possibility, they will find it. If there is a different way of doing something, they will do it. Although not all "creativity" in persons with ADHD is related to visual or performing arts, many clients I work with have this amazing **artistic** ability.

One of these creative persons with ADHD was an art major in college. The assignment for her class was to take "1000 of something" and make it into a sculpture that the 1000 things would not normally be used for. On the day the assignment was due, this student turned in shoes made entirely of flowers!

As a poor college coed, this amazingly creative ADHD student bypassed her lack of resources by asking a local flower shop if they could donate

Brain Surfing & 31 Other Awesome Qualities

flowers for her project. Much to her surprise, they ended up giving her buckets of carnations and daisies that she promptly took back to her dorm and "pressed" between the pages of her and her roommates' text books. Once dried and flattened, she then created a resin "fabric" out of the flowers and spread it to dry. From this "fabric" she made a pair of shoes using a pattern she discovered on the internet. Once the shoes were complete, she had one last dilemma...there were not 1000 flowers in her project. Using her creativity and ingenuity, this student promptly told her professor that there were, however, 1000 petals! She named the piece "He loves me, He loves me not", received an A on the project and earned a coveted spot in a local art show! Voila, ADHD creativity!

Awesome ADHD Quality #4 & #5 Fun to be With and Life of the Party

"Live life fully while you're here. Experience everything. Take care of yourself and your friends. Have fun, be crazy, be weird. Go out and screw up! You're going to anyway, so you might as well enjoy the process. Take the opportunity to learn from your mistakes: find the cause of your problem and eliminate it. Don't try to be perfect; just be an excellent example of being human."

~Anthony Robbins

Fun to be With and Life of the Party

One of the most amazing people with ADHD I know is my nephew. Throughout his life, he has had more enthusiasm than anyone I've met. Growing up, during holiday events or birthday parties, his glee about the festivities was contagious! In fact, my sister would often say that one of the ways she could make a lot of extra money would be to rent him out for parties! There's something magical about being able to brighten someone else's day just by being your own fabulous self, isn't there?

Awesome ADHD Quality #6

Sees Details Others Miss

"I never see what has been done; I only see what remains to be done."

~Marie Curie

Sees Details Others Miss

One of the seemingly contradictory facts about living with ADHD is that the obvious will be missed. For instance, a box that has been sitting for weeks, waiting to be moved, will be walked by and completely ignored. However, other minor details will be noticed or even obsessed over.

When my son was in 5th grade, he was learning the math concepts of perimeter and area. To reinforce the learning, his teacher asked the students to draw a picture of their classroom, measure the walls and determine the area and perimeter of the space.

When my husband and I came in for our parent-teacher conference, the teacher expressed concerned that my son did not understand this math principle and pulled out the picture he had drawn. Indeed, there were no answers next to "area" and "perimeter", but what grabbed our attention, was

Brain Surfing & 31 Other Awesome Qualities

the detailed picture that my son <u>had</u> drawn of his classroom.

He had drawn a picture of his classroom as if you were looking down into it from the ceiling. Each desk, cupboard, backpack, and chair was drawn in detail! I was confused by one thing…there were diagonal lines that crossed the room. When I asked about these, my son said these were the wires that hung their art projects. All together, my son's teacher, my husband and I looked up and saw two thin, nearly invisible empty wires strung from one corner of the classroom to the other, void at this time of any creative masterpieces.

Still in awe of the picture, but remembering why were there, I asked my son why he had not answered the math problems. He replied, matter-of-fact and with utmost calm, that after drawing the picture, there simply wasn't time. His amazing ADHD brain, had missed the obvious while busy seeing the world from another angle!

Awesome ADHD Quality #7
Innovative

"The most successful people are those who are good at Plan B."

~James Yorke

Innovative

Innovative, according to the *Collins English Dictionary – Complete and Unabridged*, means using or showing new methods, ideas, etc. People with ADHD are definitely "innovative"!

Over the years, some of my favorite clients have been young adults preparing to transition to college or out on their own. I will never forget the innovation one of these students used to get out of bed and to class in the mornings!

Like many people in college, waking up and getting out of bed for morning classes was a nightmare and a near impossibility. Setting alarms often failed. Having someone physically shake them out of bed was not a sure thing. One ADHD college student came up with a very innovative way of making sure he got out of bed and didn't miss any of his morning classes. Each night as he was getting ready for bed, this client would go through a routine. He would prepare the coffee to automatically go off in the morning and set the alarm by his bed. However, he knew that the alarm by his bed would seldom be enough. To solve this problem, he made sure that as he readied himself for bed each night, he set the timer on the coffee pot to go off exactly five minutes after his alarm by his bed went off. His fail-proof innovation? When he made the coffee the night before, he made sure that the coffee carafe was not under the coffee maker! If he didn't get up shortly after his bedside alarm went off, the morning coffee would end up all over the floor! According to him…it never failed. Now that's innovative!

Awesome ADHD Quality
#8
Humorous

"A sense of humor... is needed armor. Joy in one's heart and some laughter on one's lips is a sign that the person down deep has a pretty good grasp of life."
~Hugh Sidey

Humorous

Some of the funniest people I know have ADHD. Their quick wit, creativity and intelligence make them incredibly amusing in their daily life, and for some it has even led to a career!

Read the list below to see the names of some prominent comedians who have been reported to have been diagnosed with ADHD.

- Jim Carey
- Whoopi Goldberg
- Robin Williams
- Howie Mandel
- George Burns
- Bill Cosby
- Dustin Hoffman
- Suzanne Somers

Awesome ADHD Quality

#9

Inspiring

"It's kind of fun to do the impossible."

~Walt Disney

Inspiring

Having ADHD often requires the overcoming of many obstacles. Time and again I've had the pleasure of watching clients reach goals despite their challenges. Following is an inspiring story about one such client who wasn't diagnosed with ADHD until he was in his early thirties and how he achieved his goal of becoming an attorney.

Despite initially dropping out of high school, Jake (names have been changed to protect his privacy) was determined to earn a college degree. Late in his teens, he enrolled in a two-year community college and spent the next ten years of his life pursuing his two-year associate's degree. Because of the challenges from his undiagnosed ADHD, he often failed classes and had to take them over and until he passed the course. Finally, after ten years,

Jake graduated from the community college and set his sights on earning his bachelor's degree.

Now in his late 20's, with added maturity and academic experience, he managed to complete the remainder of his bachelor degree and law degree in just over four years. It was during this time that Jake was diagnosed with ADHD and was able to minimize his academic challenges with a combination of strategies, medication and a true love and interest in the law.

Today, Jake is married with two children and practicing law with a specialty in representing persons with special needs. As inspiring as his academic success is, perhaps the most amazing part of Jake's story is that he now serves on the Board of Directors of that same community college that he once struggled so long and hard to conquer. He has come full circle and is a true inspiration.

Awesome ADHD Quality #10 Resourceful

"Never trouble another for what you can do yourself."

~Thomas Jefferson

Resourceful

Another amazing quality of persons with ADHD is resourcefulness: that unique ability to make do in nearly any situation by taking advantage of what is available.

As I have said earlier, many of the people I know with ADHD are college students, struggling to endure boring lectures, stay on top of coursework and manage their time so deadlines are met.

One of the most common strategies that students with ADHD find helpful to focus when they are studying, is having some sort of music or sound in the background. This background sound might be music, a fan, the TV/radio on low, etc. In fact, I would say that nearly 90% of my clients, students or adults use this strategy when trying to keep their focus on tasks less interesting. It may not make sense that a sound playing low in the background can help persons with ADHD focus. However, what seems to happen is that the sound occupies a part of the brain that needs to keep active so another part of the brain can focus on the less interesting task. Many well-meaning parents who have spent years trying to help their student study better by confining them to a completely quiet room, are surprised by how well this strategy works!

One resourceful student told me how he discovered his best study spot…the "laundry" room of his dorm! It seemed the noise of his dorm room was too distracting and the library was too quiet. Doing laundry one day, he noticed that he had also completed a lot of his homework! For him, the hum of the machines, the pleasant warmth of the room, and the fact that it smelled good had managed to occupy that part of his brain that needed just enough distraction, making homework a breeze.

Ahhhh…the amazing resourcefulness of the ADHD brain!

Awesome ADHD Quality #11
Highly Sensitive

"When we become aware that we do not have to escape our pains, but that we can mobilize them into a common search for life, those very pains are transformed from expressions of despair into signs of hope."

~Henri Nouwen

Highly Sensitive

Another common trait that many people with ADHD share is their seemingly super-human sensory ability. Frequently, I hear stories from parents about children being bothered by seemingly insignificant noises, annoyed by either too bright or too little light or flat out refusing to eat food with certain textures. This "super" sensory or highly sensitive ability shows up in the amazing ability of some persons with ADHD to be able to feel the "tags" in their shirts or wanting to be tucked in so snuggly in their beds at night that their parents worry if they can breathe!

Whatever the reason, many people with ADHD have this super-human, amazing ability. In fact, it is so common that I often refer to it as "the wrinkle in the sock" ability! Named after, you guessed it, my own personal experience, this time with my son.

When he was younger, my son would require an exceptional amount of time in order to get ready for school. The problem? "Wrinkles" in his socks. At first, I was confused when he would go through several pairs of socks "feeling" for the right fit. What I hadn't noticed, but which his highly sensitive feet did notice, was the small seam that runs across the toes to bind the sock during manufacturing. Amazingly, through trial and error and a great degree of patience, my son had discovered pairs where the "wrinkle" did <u>not</u> exist. Happy was the day when we discovered these!

Today, the seams in my son's socks don't seem to matter, and he is perhaps one of the classiest dressers among his friends. It seems his sensitivity to textures has matured into a fine eye for fashion!

Awesome ADHD Quality #12
Able to Hyper-focus

"Ninety percent of my game is mental. It's my concentration that has gotten me this far."

~Chris Evert

Able to Hyper-focus

The counterintuitive nature of ADHD never ceases to amaze me. When most people think of the disorder, they assume people with ADHD can never pay attention, are constantly distracted or equally impulsive. The mystery is that one of the most amazing and surprising attributes of persons with ADHD is the ability to hyper-focus on something to such an extent that all else ceases to exist. The key is that it is always something that they are interested in.

One young client described this amazing quality as we were talking about the sometimes difficult time he had hearing his mom call him to dinner or to do his chores when he was reading. In fact, he described himself while he was reading a book as going into a "book coma". He would become so engrossed in the reading that he would completely tune out his mother calling to remind him to do homework, finish chores or get ready for bed. His natural interest in reading and ability to hyper-focus had him reading at a grade level way beyond his years!

I am convinced that this ability to focus exclusively on something that they are interested in has led many people with ADHD to great success. For this student, it was reading; for others, it is becoming the world's fastest swimmer or developing the theory of relativity!

Awesome ADHD Quality #13
Musically Intuitive

"Nor do I hear in my imagination the parts successively; I hear them all at once. What a delight this is! All this inventing, this producing, takes place in a pleasing, lively dream."

~Wolfgang Amadeus Mozart

Musically Intuitive

There is a general understanding that persons with ADHD are naturally right-brained and have a high level of creativity. One of the amazing qualities and strengths I see over and over again is this incredible, innate musical talent that persons with ADHD often possess.

Now, I myself play several instruments, but I am sure to explain that any ability I have is purely a result of practice accompanied by years and years of lessons. What I am talking about here, regarding persons with ADHD musical intuitiveness, is that uncanny pure genius I see with so many of my clients and their musical talent.

Over the years, I have worked with clients that have combined their computer engineering talent and sharp ear for sound and music to become some of the top DJs on the Los Angeles music scene. Others hold titles in international musical championships. One of my favorite stories about this quality for musical genius in people with ADHD, is a client who goes into such a focused zone during his guitar performances, that he actually drools!

Awesome ADHD Quality #14
Single-Minded Pursuit of a Goal

"Success in any endeavor requires single-minded attention to detail and total concentration."

~Willie Sutton

Single-Minded Pursuit of a Goal

A quality I have to include in this book is the single-minded determination and pursuit of a goal that is common among persons with ADHD. In 1993, Thomas Hartman wrote a book called "ADD - A Different Perception", that popularized this concept of the "Hunter". Hartmann theorized that persons with ADHD were genetically "Hunters" living in a modern, slower-paced "Farmers" society. According to Hartmann, most people would have needed these "Hunter" traits to survive 10,000 years ago, and while the "Farmer" types have adapted over the years, the "Hunters" retained their hunter traits. These traits included the ability to scan the environment (for prey) and to notice small changes in their environment in the event of danger or excitement (the hunt). In their world, according to Hartmann, there was little need for planning or awareness of time when survival was the goal.

When socially and culturally our species discovered the benefits of "farming", the need to plan ahead, organize and to wait (for crops to mature) became important. Not necessarily the strengths of the "Hunter" brain. Hartmann's perspective may be debatable, but his precepts ring true for many people with ADHD.

In our day, Hartmann's "Hunter" isn't necessarily looking to kill their food or fight for their survival, however many persons with ADHD still enjoy hunting for "the sale", or "the prize in sports", lands to "conquer" or "defend". When my son was growing up, I would often say that if he had 50 acres and a knife he would be just fine. Today, I am convinced that part of his "Hunter" brain is serving him well as he serves our country in the military.

Awesome ADHD Quality #15 Adventurous

"Man cannot discover new oceans unless he has the courage to lose sight of the shore."

~Andre Gide

Adventurous

In general, adventurers are in their element when they are discovering something new or experiencing something different. I am not surprised that adventurous people such as Columbus, Lewis and Clark and other explorers are now thought to have had ADHD. Who else but a person with ADHD would embark on an adventure where the end result is uncertain, the risks of death are high, each day would be unpredictable....not to mention that you might even fall off the edge of the world! But with great risk comes great reward, and people with ADHD are prime candidates for seizing opportunities that might stop others dead in their tracks.

Awesome ADHD Quality #16
Intelligent

"There are painters who transform the sun to a yellow spot, but there are others who with the help of their art and their intelligence transform a yellow spot into the sun."

~Pablo Picasso

Intelligent

One of the many reasons I love being an ADHD Coach is that I get to work with such amazingly intelligent people! Unfortunately, many diagnosed with ADHD don't perform well on current social standardized tests, so their intelligence is overlooked or misunderstood. Daily, I recognize that the intelligence of persons with ADHD cannot be measured by their GPA, standardized test scores or academic standing. Rather, persons with ADHD show their intelligence in such areas as:

- An aptitude in math, English, writing, sports, computers, visual and performing arts, nature, etc.
- Creative and productive thinking and the ability to play with ideas
- Having a sense of humor
- The willingness to take risks and tolerance for ambiguity
- The ability to become submerged (dare I say "hyper focused") in a task

Brain Surfing & 31 Other Awesome Qualities

In 1999, author Howard Gardner theorized that a minimum of eight intelligences exist and as little as two are consistently utilized in most of our current academic institutions. In his book, *Theory of Multiple Intelligences*, Gardner states that human beings have many different ways to learn and process information. His list includes the intelligence of linguistics, logic-mathematical, musical, spatial, bodily kinesthetic, the naturalist, interpersonal and intrapersonal intelligence. Gardner is considering a ninth, or existential intelligence, but has not added it yet.

Over and over again, I remind my clients that everyone's brain works a bit differently. Everyone is smart in some way and, more likely, multiple ways. And if we can discover these in ourselves, appreciate and honor and express our own natural intelligences…that, my friends, is happiness.

Awesome ADHD Quality #17 Can Talk... A Lot

"I like to do all the talking myself. It saves time, and prevents arguments."

~Oscar Wilde

Can Talk...A Lot

Another amazing quality of persons with ADHD can be their ability to talk...A LOT! Persons with ADHD are often masters at storytelling, getting things off their mind or even problem-solving by talking it through. If you don't want that uncomfortable silence that can sometimes show itself in a conversation, engage a person with ADHD. Their quickness of thought, ability to think creatively and sense of humor will often leave every question answered.

Awesome ADHD Quality #18 & #19
Multi-tasker & Productive

"Multitasking is the art of distracting yourself from two things you'd rather not be doing by doing them simultaneously."

~Author Unknown

Multi-tasker & Productive

People with ADHD can think of a lot of things…and do a lot of things…at the same time! It is truly an awesome quality! Over and over again, I hear stories of how people with ADHD are able to juggle the complexities of having multiple things going at the same time. In fact, many share that it was when life "slowed" down or they didn't have as many things to keep track of that they noticed themselves getting bored and struggling with completing even the everyday chores.

Although every person with ADHD is different, it seems that honoring the need of the ADHD brain to be kept busy is a strategy many find helpful. An example of this is when I will suggest to students to spread their homework around their dining table in "stations": history here, math there, science at the other end. Next, I will tell them to start on one and when they find themselves getting bored or stuck, to move quickly to the next, around the table, until their homework is complete.

The same is true for accomplishing the boring everyday tasks that often overtake the day of a person with ADHD. Doing several of these "chores" at one time, for instance doing the laundry while paying the bills and alternating that with cleaning the bathrooms is just enough to check all of these items off the list…AND keep the person with ADHD stimulated and satisfied!

Awesome ADHD Quality #20

Problem Solver

"Most people spend more time and energy going around problems than in trying to solve them."

~Henry Ford

Problem Solver

"Problem Solver" or "Creative Solution Strategist" needs to be a job title for persons with ADHD. Over and over again, I am delighted by my clients' ability to figure things out and design creative solutions to challenges in some of the most ingenious of ways.

One such client of mine was a young adult who was thrilled to be meeting his goal of moving out on his own. In the process, he recognized that with his new job, he needed to be sure to keep his clothes neat and tidy. Unfortunately, in the past the avoidance of this "boring" task had him dressing himself off of the floor every day. Not the impression he wanted to make in his new career.

This young "solution strategist" recognized that part of his challenge was that when he folded and put his clothes away, he would forget what he had to wear and would end up once again dressing out of his clothes hamper. Determined not to let this get in his way of his new career, this client decided that he would get rid of his dresser entirely! A strategy most would not consider a viable solution. What this client realized was that the problem was not only that the task of folding his clothes was boring and therefore kept him from keeping his clothes tidy, but that putting items in the closed drawers made it difficult for him to remember what options he had to wear. As he moved into his new apartment, he left the dresser at home, added an additional rung in his closet for all of his shirts and even used a hanging "shoe rack" to store his underwear and socks. Problem solved!

Awesome ADHD Quality #21
Able to Live in the Moment

"When we are capable of living in the moment free from the tyranny of "should", free from the nagging sensation that this moment isn't right, we will have peaceful hearts."

~Author Unknown

Able to Live in the Moment

There is a lot of focus these days about how happiness lies in our ability to "live in the moment". To forget about what has happened in the past and not worry about what might happen in the future. The ability to focus on the here and now and make these moments count. The ability to live in the moment is another one of the amazingly awesome qualities persons with ADHD naturally possess. Although there are many stories I could share here, I am most reminded of this ability to "live in the moment" with my own son.

When my kids were growing up, traveling was a part of our lives. It was common for us to drive hours in our van to visit family or friends. Each child eagerly anticipated the trips and getting ready for them was fairly routine. There was a general "things to take list", with the kids doing their major packing, and I went around before the duffle bags were zipped to make sure nothing was missed.

As we loaded into our van for one particular trip, with snacks at the ready after several days or weeks of packing and family discussion, my youngest son with ADHD asked quite nonchalantly, "Where are we going?" The first time this happened, I assumed I had been too busy to make sure he knew our destination or that he had somehow misunderstood during the talk about our upcoming trip. As I learned more about ADHD, and as he continued to ask "Where are we going?" just before leaving, I realized that for him, this was all "in the moment". The packing was "in the moment", the planning was "in the moment".

Over the years, his now-anticipated question of "Where are we going?" as he loads his bag has turned into one of our family's fondest stories. Now I can truly appreciate his unique ability to take things as they come, trust in the process and enjoy the moment.

Awesome ADHD Quality #22
Willing to Take Risks

"Only those who will risk going too far can possibly find out how far one can go."

~T.S. Elliot

Willing to Take Risks

An inordinate number of people diagnosed with ADHD choose to serve in professions that require them to put their life at risk or to step out of their comfort zone. Over the years, I have worked with Police Officers, Emergency Room Doctors, Firefighters, Paramedics and Nurses, just to name a few. Having an ADHD brain makes it uniquely possible for some people to thrive in risky situations and is therefore an awesome ADHD quality.

Personally, I believe this amazingly quality is the result of a combination of other attributes of persons with ADHD. Acting in ways that others might call "impulsive", people in these high-risk jobs are acknowledged for their "quick thinking". What some might call "distractibility" is what allows the firefighter to notice the sound of a person trapped in a back room. What some might interpret as the "inability to focus" is the amazing ability of the Emergency Room Doctor to tune out everything else that might distract him in the busy hospital except the needs of the critical patient before him on the cart.

Awesome ADHD Quality

#23

High Energy

"Passion is energy. Feel the power that comes from focusing on what excites you."
~Oprah Winfrey

High Energy

Without generalizing here, I think it can be said that many people with ADHD have a great deal more energy than the majority of the population. Labels such as "The Energizer Bunny" have been used to describe many people with the disorder. Some clients even say that it feels like they "are driven by an internal motor". Although at times persons with ADHD say that they would like to slow down, this ability to keep going and going is to be envied by those of us that might otherwise feel we are "running on empty".

Awesome ADHD Quality #24 Curious

"When you're curious, you find lots of interesting things to do."

~Walt Disney

Curious

Where would our world be without this amazing quality that is characteristic of persons with ADHD? This quality accounts for so many new discoveries and inventions.

This ADHD characteristic to ask "why" or "what" or "how" or "when" has resulted in many marvelous technological, medical and geographic advances and understanding.

Below is a list of some of the more famous "curious" people thought to have ADHD:

- Albert Einstein
- Thomas Edison
- Alexander Graham Bell
- Benjamin Franklin
- Orville & Wilber Wright
- Henry Ford
- Bill Gates

Awesome ADHD Quality #25 Imaginative

"The true sign of intelligence is not knowledge but imagination."

~Albert Einstein

Imaginative

Without a doubt, one of the world's most imaginative minds was Walt Disney. Although never officially diagnosed, it is understood that Walt Disney had ADHD. As a film producer, director, animator, entertainer, screenwriter and more, his imagination changed the possibilities of the entertainment world forever.

I see this quality of imagination in many of my clients. I recognize it when they create animation movies from their Lego characters, or use a coffee pot as an alarm clock, or tell me that if I want to get a tortoise but don't want to worry about my children having to inherit it when I die, that I simply need to "Get an 'old' turtle, Coach Laurie."

My world, your world and no doubt the world would be much less colorful, exiting and interesting if people with ADHD did not have this amazing quality of imagination to share with the rest of us!

Awesome ADHD Quality #26 & #27 Tenacious & Resilient

"The most difficult thing is the decision to act, the rest is merely tenacity. The fears are paper tigers. You can do anything you decide to do. You can act to change and control your life; and the procedure, the process is its own reward."

~Amelia Earhart

Tenacious & Resilient

One of the common analogies used by persons living with ADHD to describe their challenges is that it is like constantly hitting your head against a wall. Yet despite these daily, and sometimes hourly, struggles, they continue to persevere toward their goals, determined to reach them despite the many obstacles that seem to be in their path. Yep, tenacity and resilience are two more amazing ADHD qualities. The following is only one story of a very tenacious and resilient person with ADHD.

One of my clients, a 27-year-old woman was pursuing a career as a Pediatric Nurse Practitioner. When we met, she explained that she had barely passed high school and had failed out of two colleges before discovering that she struggled with ADHD. However, in less than one year, through the use of medication and academic strategies we have designed specifically for her learning style, she has gone from a GPA of 1.7 to a GPA of 3.5!

I am constantly amazed and inspired by her firm resolve to reach her dream despite consistent feedback from family, peers and instructors telling her she should set her sights a bit lower. One of my greatest pleasures in this last year was to write her a letter of recommendation to nursing school. As a nurse myself, I know that her persistence, determination and unwavering commitment to reach her goal will serve her patients well when she achieves her dream of becoming a Nurse Practitioner. And I will be loudly cheering her on every step of the way!

Awesome ADHD Quality #28
Unique

"There is only one of you in all time, this expression is unique. And if you block it, it will never exist through any other medium and it will be lost."

~Martha Graham

Unique

When people ask me what it is like to coach people with ADHD, I often tell them it is a bit like being a treasure hunter. Each and every day, I help people uncover their amazing qualities and discover their own multi-faceted inherent value.

Although it is true that people diagnosed with ADHD have similar core symptoms, the uniqueness and individuality of each person is remarkable! An analogy I use to describe what ADHD is like for different people is this:

Every person has two eyes, two ears, one nose, mouth, chin, two eyebrows, etc., but it is how they individually and uniquely come together on our face that makes each of us look a bit different from one another. Persons with ADHD are the same. Their strengths, challenges, motivators, personality, interests, etc., are all wrapped up to make each unique individual. This amazingly colorful package, in my opinion, shines more brightly and is more precious than what they might be like without their ADHD.

Awesome ADHD Quality #29
Good Negotiator

"Negotiating techniques do not work all that well with kids, because in the middle of a negotiation, they will say something completely unrelated such as, 'You know what? I have a belly button!' and completely throw you off guard."

~Bo Bennett

Good Negotiator

Perhaps debatable (pun intended) is whether or not being a keen negotiator is an "awesome quality" of ADHD. Parents raising ADHD children complain about being "worn out" by their children negotiating everything from bedtime to baseball. However, being a good negotiator can lead to lucrative careers in business, law and politics. In fact, many of my adult clients have chosen these careers.

Being able to persuade someone to see your point of view, change their mind and give you what you want is an enviable life skill. If you are a parent reading this, I ask you to consider that this quality can serve your child well as they head into adulthood. Be patient and encourage your child to develop additional negotiator qualities such as the skill of listening and being gracious if the outcome doesn't necessarily go their way. Who knows, one day they might be negotiating on your behalf!

Awesome ADHD Quality #30

Charming

"Charm is a glow that casts a most becoming light on others."

~John Mason Brown

Charming

One of the adjectives used to describe many people with ADHD is charming. Whatever magic makes up the attraction, people with ADHD have this amazing quality in abundance.

Being an ADHD Coach I am lucky to spend my days with these charmers. However, one person stands out in particular. His name was Ken Zaretzky, Senior Certified ADHD Coach. Ken was one of the founders of ADHD Coaching, proud of his ADHD and a fierce advocate for persons living with the disorder. Ken possessed a unique charm and had a personality that was "larger than life".

Whenever Ken would enter a room, you knew it, because he walked in with his shoulders back and head held high as if to say "Here I am!" If you happened to walk into a room that Ken was in, he would acknowledge and greet you with a loud voice and warm smile as if to say "There you are!" His interest in his clients, colleagues and family was genuine, gentle and sincere. It was not possible to leave a conversation with him and not feel better about yourself.

Unfortunately, my good friend and colleague, Ken, passed away unexpectedly in February 2011. It is a loss to all of us who knew him and those he did not yet have the opportunity to meet. He will be greatly missed by me and the ADHD community. Here's to you, Ken!

Awesome ADHD Quality #31 & #32
Never Bored & Never Boring

"When I find myself getting bored, I like to drive downtown and get a great parking spot, then sit in my car and count how many people ask me if I'm leaving."

~Stephen Wright

Never Bored & Never Boring

Last, but certainly not least, the final two amazing qualities of persons with ADHD are that they are never bored and never boring. Poorly organized, inconsistent, late...but never boring!

As a frequent speaker on ADHD and Coaching, I have the pleasure of attending many events and conferences about ADHD. If you want to have the best time of your life, discover your tribe and feel right at home, all you need to do is attend a conference that focuses on ADHD.

Pause for a moment and imagine a hotel filled with hundreds of people with ADHD. Events and conferences filled with people of varying interests, spontaneity, imagination, adventurousness, intelligence, enthusiasm, and creativity...you can't help but have a great time and then leave inspired and ready to take on the world!

In parting, I want to leave you with this final thought:

ADHD does present challenges and struggles for people who have been diagnosed with the disorder. However, having ADHD is not only about negative behaviors needing to be fixed. With better understanding of your ADHD, learning new strategies and techniques to more effectively manage areas where ADHD is a challenge for you, it can free you and those you love to enjoy the other amazing and awesome qualities of your ADHD!

Warmly,

Laurie

Want to find out more about ADHD and how you can use some of your amazing strengths and positive qualities to create a life of success, happiness and fulfillment?

Visit me at:
www.CoachingforADHD.com

Want to tell others about your positive ADHD qualities? "Like" me on Facebook at:

www.facebook.com/CoachingforADHD

Want to work directly with Laurie Dupar? Schedule a 15 minute get-acquainted session with Laurie today to find out if ADHD coaching is right for you.

Go to:
www.CoachingforADHD.com

or email:

Laurie@CoachingforADHD.com

I look forward to hearing from you!

~Laurie

www.ingramcontent.com/pod-product-compliance
Lightning Source LLC
Chambersburg PA
CBHW071707040426
42446CB00011B/1952